# A Mind Unbound:
## The Story of Mary Shelley

Mary Wollstonecraft Shelley was born into a family of radical thinkers and writers in Somers Town, London, on August 30, 1797. Her parents, Mary Wollstonecraft and William Godwin, were both prominent writers and thinkers of their time. Her mother, Mary Wollstonecraft, was a pioneering feminist and author of "A Vindication of the Rights of Woman," a seminal work in the field of women's rights. Her father, William Godwin, was a philosopher and political radical who espoused the idea of anarchism.

Unfortunately, Mary's mother died just days after her birth, leaving her father to raise her and her half-sister, Fanny Imlay. Despite the loss of her mother, Mary grew up in a stimulating intellectual environment, surrounded by her father's circle of friends, which included Samuel Taylor Coleridge, Charles Lamb, and William Wordsworth. Her father's library was a treasure trove of books on philosophy, politics, and literature, which Mary eagerly devoured from an early age.

However, Mary's childhood was not without its challenges. Her father's financial difficulties and his radical politics meant that the family was often on the move and struggled to make ends meet.

Mary was sent to live with family friends in Scotland for a time, and later attended a boarding school in Wales, where she was often lonely and isolated.

Despite these challenges, Mary's early life was marked by a sense of curiosity and a desire to learn. She was fascinated by science and the natural world, and spent hours exploring the countryside and collecting specimens. Her imagination was also sparked by the stories and legends she heard from her father and his friends.

Mary's early life and childhood set the stage for her later achievements as a writer and thinker. Her exposure to radical ideas and her intellectual curiosity were integral to the development of her own ideas and writing.

## Meeting Percy Bysshe Shelley

As Mary Shelley entered adulthood, she found herself drawn to the literary and intellectual circles of London. It was there that she met the man who would become both her greatest love and her greatest muse: Percy Bysshe Shelley.

Shelley was a rising star in the literary world, known for his radical political views and his passionate poetry.

Mary was immediately captivated by his
intelligence and his fiery spirit,
and the two quickly fell in love.

Their relationship was not without its
challenges, however. Shelley was still married
to his first wife, and his political views made
him a controversial figure in society. Despite
these obstacles, Mary and Percy continued to see
each other in secret, and their love affair
deepened with each passing day.

As their relationship blossomed, Mary and Percy
began to collaborate on a number of creative
projects. They shared a deep love of literature
and philosophy, and their conversations were
often filled with passionate debates about the
nature of humanity and the meaning of existence.

In 1814, Mary and Percy eloped to Europe
together, along with Mary's stepsister Claire
Clairmont. The trip would prove to be a turning
point in Mary's life, inspiring her to write one
of the most influential works of science fiction
in history: Frankenstein.

## Frankenstein and its Publication

Mary had traveled to Switzerland with her lover,
the poet Percy Bysshe Shelley, and their friend
Lord Byron. It was there, in the midst of a rainy
summer, that the idea for Frankenstein was born.

The group passed the time by reading ghost stories and discussing the latest scientific theories, including the work of Luigi Galvani, who had discovered the principles of electricity and muscle movement.

One evening, as they discussed the possibility of bringing a corpse back to life through electricity, Byron proposed that each of them write a ghost story. It was a challenge that Mary initially struggled with, but after a few sleepless nights, the idea for Frankenstein came to her.

The novel tells the story of a young scientist named Victor Frankenstein who, driven by a desire for knowledge and power, creates a living being from dead body parts. The creature, rejected by its creator and shunned by society, turns to violence and revenge.

Despite the controversial subject matter, Mary was determined to publish her novel. She found a publisher in the small firm of Lackington, Hughes, Harding, Mavor & Jones, and the first edition of Frankenstein was published anonymously in 1818. The novel was an instant success, and critics hailed it as a masterpiece of Gothic horror and Romantic literature.

Over the years, Frankenstein has become one of the most iconic and influential works in the English language. It has been adapted countless times for stage, screen, and even ballet, and its themes of science, ambition, and the human condition continue to resonate with readers today. Mary Shelley's novel has truly become a timeless classic, and its enduring popularity is a testament to the power of her imagination and the lasting impact of her literary legacy.

## The Shelleys in Italy

Mary Shelley and her husband, Percy, spent several years living in Italy, a period that was marked by a mix of personal joy and professional struggle. The couple first arrived in Italy in 1818, accompanied by their young son, William, and a handful of friends. Italy provided them a more liberal and politically tolerant atmosphere compared to England at the time.

During their time in Pisa, the Shelleys rented a villa which became a hub of intellectual and artistic activity. The group of friends, which also included Edward Trelawny and Leigh Hunt, spent their days discussing literature, philosophy, and politics. They also engaged in various creative pursuits, with Mary Shelley working on her novel "Mathilda," and Percy Shelley producing some of his most famous works, including "Prometheus Unbound."

Despite the intellectual stimulation and camaraderie, the period was not without its struggles. The Shelleys' financial situation was precarious, and they often found themselves in debt. They relied on loans and financial support from friends and family, and Percy Shelley's refusal to inherit his family's fortune added to their financial struggles. They were also plagued by personal tragedies, including the death of their son, William, and Mary's subsequent miscarriage.

In 1822, tragedy would strike again when Percy drowned in a boating accident off the coast of Italy. Mary was devastated by his death and struggled to cope with the loss of her husband and the father of her children. She remained in Italy for some time, dealing with the legal and financial aftermath of Percy's death and continuing to write.

After her husband's death, Mary Shelley returned to England with their surviving son, Percy Florence Shelley. She continued to write and publish throughout her life, but she never forgot her time in Italy and the friends and experiences that she had there. In many ways, her time in Italy was a formative period that shaped both her personal and professional life.

# Themes and Ideas Explored in Mary Shelley's Prominent Works

Mary Shelley's ideas and philosophy were heavily influenced by the intellectual and social environment she grew up in and the events that occurred throughout her life. She was deeply interested in the human condition, exploring themes such as creation, responsibility, identity, and the search for meaning in her writing. Her works often challenge conventional notions of morality, gender, and power, and she was a strong advocate for social justice and equality.

In "Frankenstein" (1818), Shelley grapples with the idea of creation and the responsibility that comes with it. Through the character of Victor Frankenstein, she questions the consequences of playing God and the ethical implications of scientific progress. She also delves into themes of isolation and the search for identity, as the monster struggles to find his place in the world and understand his own existence.

In "Valperga" (1823), Shelley delves into the theme of power and its corrupting influence. Set in medieval Italy, the novel follows the struggles for power and control between two opposing factions.

Shelley challenges traditional notions of gender and power, depicting strong female characters who are not afraid to take charge and challenge the status quo.

"The Last Man" (1826) contemplates mortality and the fleeting nature of human life. Set in a post-apocalyptic world, the novel follows the last survivor of a deadly plague as he grapples with the meaning of his own existence and the loss of all he has ever known. Through this story, Shelley raises questions about the nature of human existence and the purpose of life.

"Lodore" (1835) examines the theme of motherhood and the challenges faced by women in a patriarchal society. The novel follows the story of a young woman who is forced to navigate the expectations and demands of society as she raises her child alone. Shelley advocates for women's rights and challenges traditional gender roles, depicting women as strong and capable individuals who are not defined solely by their roles as wives and mothers.

"Mathilda" (published posthumously in 1959) explores the taboo subjects of incest and suicide. The novel follows the story of a young woman who is haunted by the memory of her father's inappropriate affections and ultimately takes her own life. Shelley uses this story to raise questions about the role of society in shaping individual identity and the psychological effects of trauma and abuse.

# Later Years and Legacy

As Mary Shelley entered her later years, she began to suffer from a variety of illnesses, including migraines, respiratory problems, and what may have been a brain tumor. Despite her health challenges, she continued to write and publish, though her later works received less critical acclaim than her earlier ones.

Sadly, Mary Shelley's health continued to decline, and she passed away on February 1, 1851, at the age of 53. She was buried at St. Peter's Church in Bournemouth, England, alongside her parents and husband.

Her most famous novel, Frankenstein, has become a cultural icon and continues to inspire adaptations, reimaginings, and scholarly analyses. In addition, Mary Shelley's life and work have served as an inspiration to generations of writers, particularly women writers, who have been inspired by her tenacity, creativity, and willingness to challenge societal norms.

Though Mary Shelley faced numerous challenges and setbacks throughout her life, she remained committed to her craft and her beliefs, leaving behind a rich legacy that has endured for centuries. Her life and work continue to inspire and captivate readers, and her impact on literature and society is felt to this day.

A truce to philosophy!
— Life is before me
and I rush into
possession.
Hope, glory, love, and
blameless ambition
are my guides, and my
soul knows no dread.


('The Last Man')

Did you not call this a
glorious expedition? and
wherefore was it glorious? not
because the way was smooth and
placid as a southern sea, but
because it was full of dangers
and terror, because at every
new incident your fortitude
was to be called forth and your
courage exhibited, because
danger and death surrounded
it, and these you were brave to
overcome. for this was it a
glorious, for this was it an
honorable undertaking


('Frankenstein')

With how many things
are we on the brink
of becoming
acquainted,
if cowardice or
carelessness
did not restrain
our inquiries.

('Frankenstein')

If the study to which
you apply yourself has
a tendency to weaken
your affections and to
destroy your taste for
those simple pleasures
in which no alloy can
possibly mix, then that
study is certainly
unlawful, that is to
say, not befitting the
human mind.


('Frankenstein')

None knew of their love except
their own two hearts. It was
pure and unsophisticated:
it had the poetry of an early
world, when the materials of
our feelings were not yet cast
in the strong mould of
circumstances, and men
wandered forth, like children,
in the universe that lay before
them, to gather knowledge from
every thing lovely or majestic;
and, if danger rose, to seek
shelter in the bosom of love.


('Mathilda')

A human being in
perfection ought
always to preserve
a calm and peaceful
mind and never to
allow passion or a
transitory desire to
disturb his
tranquility.

('Frankenstein')

Heavy misfortunes have befallen us, but let us only cling closer to what remains, and transfer our love for those whom we have lost to those who yet live. Our circle will be small, but bound close by the ties of affection and mutual misfortune. And when time shall have softened your despair, new and dear objects of care will be born to replace those of whom we have been so cruelly deprived.

('Frankenstein')

As a child I scribbled; and my favourite pastime, during the hours given me for recreation, was to "write stories." Still I had a dearer pleasure than this, which was the formation of castles in the air—the indulging in waking dreams—the following up trains of thought, which had for their subject the formation of a succession of imaginary incidents. My dreams were at once more fantastic and agreeable than my writings.

('Introduction to the 1831 edition of Frankenstein')

Our feelings probably are not less strong at fifty than they were ten or fifteen years before; but they have changed their objects, and dwell on far different prospects. At five-and-thirty a man thinks of what his own existence is; when the maturity of age has grown into its autumn, he is wrapt up in that of others. The loss of wife or child then becomes more deplorable, as being impossible to repair; for no fresh connection can give us back the companion of our earlier years, nor a "new-sprung race" compensate for that, whose career we hoped to see run.

('Lodore')

But her's was the
misery of innocence,
which, like a cloud
that passes over the
fair moon, for a while
hides, but cannot
tarnish its
brightness.


('Frankenstein')

I saw no cause for their
unhappiness, but I was
deeply affected by it.
If such lovely creatures
were miserable, it was
less strange that I, an
imperfect and solitary
being, should be
wretched.


('Frankenstein')

A mind of moderate capacity which closely pursues one study must infallibly arrive at great proficiency in that study.


('Frankenstein')

...if I see but one smile
on your lips when we
meet, occasioned by
this or any other
exertion of mine, I
shall need no other
happiness.


('Frankenstein')

Man...how ignorant
art thou in thy
pride of wisdom!

('Frankenstein')

...we are unfashioned creatures, but half made up, if one wiser, better, dearer than ourselves — such a friend ought to be — do not lend his aid to perfectionate our weak and faulty natures.

('Frankenstein')

Invention, it must be
humbly admitted, does
not consist in creating
out of void, but out of
chaos.


('Frankenstein')

But he found that a traveller's life is one that includes much pain amidst its enjoyments. His feelings are for ever on the stretch; and when he begins to sink into repose, he finds himself obliged to quit that on which he rests in pleasure for something new, which again engages his attention, and which also he forsakes for other novelties.

('Frankenstein')

Oh! grief is fantastic; it weaves a web on which to trace the history of its woe from every form and change around; it incorporates itself with all living nature; it finds sustenance in every object; as light, it fills all things, and, like light, it gives its own colors to all.

('The Last Man')

The careful rearer of
the ductile human
plant can instil his
own religion, and
surround the soul
by such a moral
atmosphere, as shall
become to its latest
day the air it
breathes.


('Lodore')

You seek for
knowledge and wisdom
as I once did; and I
ardently hope that
the gratification of
your wishes may not
be a serpent to sting
you, as mine has been.


('Frankenstein')

I felt emotions of
gentleness and pleasure,
that had long appeared
dead, revive within me.
Half surprised by the
novelty of these
sensations, I allowed
myself to be borne away
by them, and forgetting
my solitude and
deformity, dared to be
happy.


('Frankenstein')

We could almost believe that we are destined by Providence to an unsettled position on the globe, so invariably is a love of change implanted in the young. It seems as if the eternal Lawgiver intended that, at a certain age, man should leave father, mother, and the dwelling of his infancy, to seek his fortunes over the wide world.

('Lodore')

Frankness and truth
were reflected on her
brow, like flowers in
the clearest pool.

('Lodore')

Men become cannibals
of their own hearts;
remorse, regret, and
restless impatience
usurp the place of
more wholesome
feeling: every thing
seems better than
that which is.


('Lodore')

I shall commit my
thoughts to paper, it
is true; but that is a
poor medium for the
communication of
feeling. I desire the
company of a man who
could sympathize
with me, whose eyes
would reply to mine.


('Frankenstein')

My proud step was no interpreter of my heart, for I deeply felt that, though surrounded by every luxury, I was a beggar.

('Transformation')

It is true, we shall be monsters, cut off from all the world; but on that account we shall be more attached to one another.

('Frankenstein')

If pain can
purify the heart,
mine will be
pure.

('Mathilda')

The whole series of my
life appeared to me as
a dream; I sometimes
doubted if indeed it
were all true, for it
never presented itself
to my mind with the
force of reality.


('Frankenstein')

Believe me, I will
never desert life until
this last hope is torn
from my bosom, that in
some way my labours
may form a link of gold
with which we ought
all to strive to drag
Happiness from where
she sits enthroned
above the clouds, now
far beyond our reach,
to inhabit the earth
with us.


('Mathilda')

Nothing is more
painful to the human
mind than, after the
feelings have been
worked up by a quick
succession of events,
the dead calmness of
inaction and certainty
which follows and
deprives the soul both
of hope and fear.


('Frankenstein')

It was the part of a
woman so to refine
and educate her mind,
as to be the cause of
good alone to him
whose fate depended
on her smile.

('Lodore')

My companion must be
of the same species, and
have the same defects...
with whom I can live in
the interchange of
those sympathies
necessary for my
being...


('Frankenstein')

Life, although it may
only be an accumulation
of anguish, is dear to me,
and I will defend it.


('Frankenstein')

Everything must have a beginning, to speak in Sanchean phrase; and that beginning must be linked to something that went before. The Hindus give the world an elephant to support it, but they make the elephant stand upon a tortoise.

('Frankenstein')

Believe me, if you
beheld on lips with
grief one smile of joy
and gratitude, and knew
that you were parent of
that smile and that
without you it had
never been, you would
feel so pure and warm a
happiness that you'd
wish to live forever
again and again to enjoy
the same pleasure.


('Mathilda')

The different accidents of life are not so changeable as the feelings of human nature. I had worked hard for nearly two years, for the sole purpose of infusing life into an inanimate body. For this I had deprived myself of rest and health. I had desired it with an ardour that far exceeded moderation; but now that I had finished, the beauty of the dream vanished, and breathless horror and disgust filled my heart.

('Frankenstein')

The young are always
in extremes; they are
either better or worse
than they appear to be;
their virtues are more
glowing, their vices
more deeply dyed;
their happiness is as
exquisite as their
misery is acute.

('Lodore')

Marriage is
usually considered
the grave, and not
the cradle of love.


('The Last Man')

I do know that for
the sympathy of one
living being, I would
make peace with all.
I have love in me the
likes of which you
can scarcely imagine
and rage the likes of
which you would not
believe. If I cannot
satisfy the one, I
will indulge the
other.


('Frankenstein')

We have had over-much
of war: I have seen too
many of the noble,
young, and gallant,
fall by the sword.
Brute force has had
its day; now let us try
what policy can do.


('The Fortunes of Perkin
Warbeck')

Precious attribute of
woe-worn humanity!
that can snatch
ecstatic emotion, even
from under the very
share and harrow, that
ruthlessly ploughs up
and lays waste every
hope.


('The Last Man')

Nothing is so painful
to the human mind as
a great and sudden
change.


('Frankenstein')

Ah! it is well for
the unfortunate to
be resigned, but for
the guilty there is
no peace.


('Frankenstein')

If our impulses were
confined to hunger,
thirst, and desire, we
might be nearly free;
but now we are moved by
every wind that blows
and a chance word or
scene that that word
may convey to us.


('Frankenstein')

Curiosity, earnest
research to learn the
hidden laws of nature,
gladness akin to
rapture, as they
unfolded to me, are
among the earliest
sensations I can
remember.


('Frankenstein')

Beware; for I am
fearless, and
therefore
powerful.


('Frankenstein')

My dreams were all my own; I accounted for them to nobody; they were my refuge when annoyed — my dearest pleasure when free.

('Introduction to the 1831 edition of Frankenstein')

Seek happiness in
tranquility and avoid
ambition even if it be
only the apparently
innocent one of
distinguishing
yourself in science
and discoveries.


('Frankenstein')

What is there so
fearful as the
expectation of evil
tidings delayed? ...
Misery is a more
welcome visitant
when she comes in
her darkest guise
and wraps us in
perpetual black, for
then the heart no
longer sickens with
disappointed hope.


('The Evil Eye')

Thus strangely are our
souls constructed,
and by such slight
ligaments are we bound
to prosperity or ruin –
an accident, perhaps as
these ligaments are, may
be the destruction of
our happiness. Under
the guidance of an
infallible Providence,
in the fullness of time,
that which is best for
us shall be revealed.


('Frankenstein')

The very winds whispered in soothing accents, and maternal Nature bade me weep no more.

('Frankenstein')

It is a strange feeling
for a girl when first she
finds the power put into
her hand of influencing
the destiny of another to
happiness or misery.
She is like a magician
holding for the first
time a fairy wand,
not having yet had
experience of its
potency.

('Lodore')

It may...be judged
indecent in me to come
forward on this occasion;
but when I see a fellow-
creature about to perish
through the cowardice of
her pretended friends,
I wish to be allowed to
speak, that I may say what
I know of her character.


('Frankenstein')

None but those who have experienced them can conceive of the enticements of science. In other studies you go as far as other have gone before you, and there is nothing more to know; but in a scientific pursuit there is continual food for discovery and wonder.

('Frankenstein')

His science was simply
human and human
science, I soon
convinced myself,
could never conquer
nature's laws so far as
to imprison the soul.


('The Last Man')

How dangerous is
the acquirement of
knowledge and how
much happier that
man is who believes
his native town to be
the world, than he
who aspires to be
greater than his
nature will allow.


('Frankenstein')

A lofty sense of
independence is,
in man, the best
privilege of his
nature.


('Lodore')

The labours of men
of genius, however
erroneously directed,
scarcely ever fail in
ultimately turning to
the solid advantage of
mankind.

('Frankenstein')

My heart was
fashioned to be
susceptible of love
and sympathy, and
when wrenched by
misery to vice and
hatred, it did not
endure the violence
of the change without
torture such as you
cannot even imagine.


('Frankenstein')

Of what a strange
nature is knowledge!
It clings to a mind
when it has once
seized on it like a
lichen on a rock.


('Frankenstein')

We never do what we
wish when we wish it,
and when we desire a
thing earnestly, and
it does arrive, that
or we are changed, so
that we slide from the
summit of our wishes
and find ourselves
where we were.


('Selected letters')

Solitude was my only
consolation - deep,
dark, deathlike
solitude.

('Frankenstein')

Ennui, the demon, waited at the threshold of his noiseless refuge, and drove away the stirring hopes and enlivening expectations, which form the better part of life.

('Lodore')

I feel exquisite
pleasure in dwelling
on the recollections of
childhood, before
misfortune had tainted
my mind, and changed
its bright visions of
extensive usefulness
into gloomy and narrow
reflections upon self.


('Frankenstein')

Listen to me,
Frankenstein. You
accuse me of murder;
and yet you would,
with a satisfied
conscience, destroy
your own creature.
Oh, praise the
eternal justice of
man!


('Frankenstein')

Nothing contributes
so much to tranquilize
the mind as a steady
purpose – a point on
which the soul may fix
its intellectual eye.


('Frankenstein')

When I run over the frightful catalogue of my sins, I cannot believe that I am the same creature whose thoughts were once filled with sublime and transcendent visions of the beauty and the majesty of goodness. But it is even so; the fallen angel becomes a malignant devil.

('Frankenstein')

I busied myself to think of a story, — a story to rival those which had excited us to this task. One which would speak to the mysterious fears of our nature, and awaken thrilling horror—one to make the reader dread to look round, to curdle the blood, and quicken the beatings of the heart. If I did not accomplish these things, my ghost story would be unworthy of its name.

('Introduction to the 1831 edition of Frankenstein')

In the evening Hogg
comes. I like him better
each time; it is a pity
that he is a lawyer; he
wasted so much time on
that trash that might be
spent on better things.


('The Life & Letters of Mary
Wollstonecraft Shelley (1889)')

The instructor can scarcely give sensibility where it is essentially wanting, nor talent to the unpercipient block. But he can cultivate and direct the affections of the pupil, who puts forth, as a parasite, tendrils by which to cling, not knowing to what – to a supporter or a destroyer.

('Lodore')

Our faults are apt
to assume giant and
exaggerated forms to
our eyes in youth; and
at that time of life we
are not always patient
under them, or disposed
to take a calm and
sober survey of the
degree of culpability
that may attach to our
own errors.


('Lodore')

There is something at work
in my soul which I do not
understand. I am practically
industrious — painstaking,
a workman to execute with
perseverance and labour —
but besides this there is a
love for the marvellous, a
belief in the marvellous,
intertwined in all my
projects, which hurries me
out of the common pathways of
men, even to the wild sea and
unvisited regions I am about
to explore.


('Frankenstein')

Invention consists in
the capacity of seizing
on the capabilities of
a subject, and in the
power of moulding and
fashioning ideas
suggested to it.


('Frankenstein')

Even where the affections are not strongly moved by any superior excellence, the companions of our childhood always possess a certain power over our minds which hardly any later friend can obtain. They know our infantine dispositions, which, however they may be afterwards modified, are never eradicated; and they can judge of our actions with more certain conclusions as to the integrity of our motives.


('Frankenstein')

My greatest pleasure was the enjoyment of a serene sky amidst these verdant woods: yet I loved all the changes of Nature; and rain, and storm, and the beautiful clouds of heaven brought their delights with them. When rocked by the waves of the lake my spirits rose in triumph as a horseman feels with pride the motions of his high fed steed.
But my pleasures arose from the contemplation of nature alone, I had no companion: my warm affections finding no return from any other human heart were forced to run waste on inanimate objects.


('Mathilda')

What are we, the
inhabitants of this
globe, least among
the many that people
infinite space?
Our minds embrace
infinity; the visible
mechanism of our
being is subject to
merest accident.


('The Last Man')

Thus far I have gone,
tracking a secure way
over the pathless seas:
the very stars themselves
being witnesses and
testimonies of my
triumph...What can stop
the determined heart and
resolved will of man?


('Frankenstein')

I was benevolent and
good; misery made me
a fiend. Make me
happy, and I shall
again be virtuous.


('Frankenstein')

Even broken in spirit as he is,
no one can feel more deeply than
he does the beauties of nature.
The starry sky, the sea, and
every sight afforded by these
wonderful regions, seems still
to have the power of elevating
his soul from earth. Such a man
has a double existence:
he may suffer misery, and be
overwhelmed by disappointments;
yet, when he has retired into
himself, he will be like a
celestial spirit that has a halo
around him, within whose circle
no grief or folly ventures.


('Frankenstein')

Revenge! — the
word seemed balm
to me; I hugged it,
caressed it, till,
like a serpent,
it stung me.


('Transformation')

I saw and heard of
none like me. Was I
then a monster, a blot
upon the earth, from
which all men fled,
and whom all men
disowned?


('Frankenstein')

To examine the causes
of life, we must first
have recourse to
death.


('Frankenstein')

Look forward to future years, if not with eager anticipation, yet with a calm reliance upon the power of good, wholly remote from despair.

('Lodore')

The moon gazed on my
midnight labours, while,
with unrelaxed and
breathless eagerness,
I pursued nature to her
hiding places.


('Frankenstein')

At the age of twenty
six I am in the
condition of an aged
person – all my old
friends are gone... &
my heart fails when I
think by how few ties
I hold to the world.


('Journal –15 May 1824')

Truly disappointment
is the guardian deity
of human life; she
sits at the threshold
of unborn time, and
marshals the events
as they come forth.


('The Last Man')

And the violet lay
dead while the odour
flew On the wings of
the wind o'er the
waters blue.


('Frankenstein')

When falsehood can
look so like the truth,
who can assure
themselves of certain
happiness?


('Frankenstein')

Happiness is in its
highest degree the
sister of goodness.


('The Last Man')

She was no longer that
happy creature who in
earlier youth wandered
with me on the banks of
the lake and talked with
ecstasy of our future
prospects. The first of
those sorrows which are
sent to wean us from the
earth had visited her,
and its dimming
influence quenched
her dearest smiles.


('Frankenstein')

A man would make but a
very sorry chemist
if he attended to that
department of human
knowledge alone. If
your wish is to become
really a man of science,
and not merely a petty
experimentalist,
I should advise you to
apply to every branch
of natural philosophy,
including mathematics.


('Frankenstein')

How mutable are our
feelings, and how
strange is that
clinging love we
have of life even in
the excess of misery!


('Frankenstein')

I could not understand
why men who knew all
about good and evil
could hate and kill
each other.


('Frankenstein')

Live, and be happy,
and make others so...
To be resigned when
suffering is hopeless,
is to be weak; to be
resigned when hope
remains, is to be a
victim. Let us then be
up and doing, and see
what the world will
come to when we have
set it to rights.


('Lodore')

Even the eternal
skies weep, I thought;
is there any shame
then, that mortal man
should spend himself
in tears?

('The Last Man')